NATURAL INGREDIENTS

Taste of the Falklands

Photographer/Designer **Julie Bellhouse**

Restaurateur **Alex Olmedo**

Saunders Island (This page); Pebble Island (Previous page)

Acknowledgements

From Alex,

To my mother Toyita, thank you for being my mamita.

Writing and developing recipes takes a lot of time and effort and without the help of my Head Chef, Sebastian Poll it would not have been possible to complete my part of the project; to him my most grateful thanks for preparing all the food featured in the book. Fellow chefs, Ricky Gana and Rodrigo Marin for their assistance and front of house, assistant manager Vanessa Ramirez.

My thanks also go to my business partners Jan Cheek and Stuart Wallace for believing in me when I created the Falklands Brasserie; without their support I would not have been able to develop my idea.

Finally, I would like to thank Julie Bellhouse for being as passionate as I am about our work, for her dedication, attention to detail and love she feels for the country we live in.

From Julie,

A special thank you to my wonderful children Jessica, Emma and Torin who have put up with my endless late nights going over photos and designing this book. To my sweetheart, Jeff Halliday who has always been there to bounce ideas off, give practical advice, encouragement and tons of support, not to mention driving me all over the Islands! Alex, without your faith in both our abilities, your generosity and your brilliant sense of style this book would not have been created. My grateful thanks to all of the people who generously let me photograph their world.

The authors would like to thank:

Falkland Islands Development Corporation; Julian and Amanda Morris for their enthusiam and encouragement; Seafish Chandlery, Falkland Islands Community School and the cookery competition competitors; and the finishing touches from the proof readers.

First published in the Falklands in May 2007 by Studio 52° and The Falklands Brasserie, Stanley, Falkland Islands FIQQ1ZZ

© Copyright photography 2007 Studio 52°   © Copyright recipes 2007 The Falklands Brasserie

ISBN: 978-0-9555538-0-6

Concept, design and layout by Studio 52°, Dean Street, Stanley, Falkland Islands FIQQ1ZZ

Photographer and designer: Julie Bellhouse

Recipe developer: Alex Olmedo

Food preparation for photography: Sebastian Poll Yurjevic

Proof readers: Jan Cheek, Sue Gyford and Lisa Johnston

Printed in Chile

Set in Frutiger, Fairfield and Corinthia

www.atasteofthefalklands.com

Contents

Starters

Mains

Desserts

Additional recipes

Sebastian dressing the spaghetti. (Left) Cookery competitor John Maskell-Bott preparing his winning dish. (Right)

FALKLAND ISLANDS

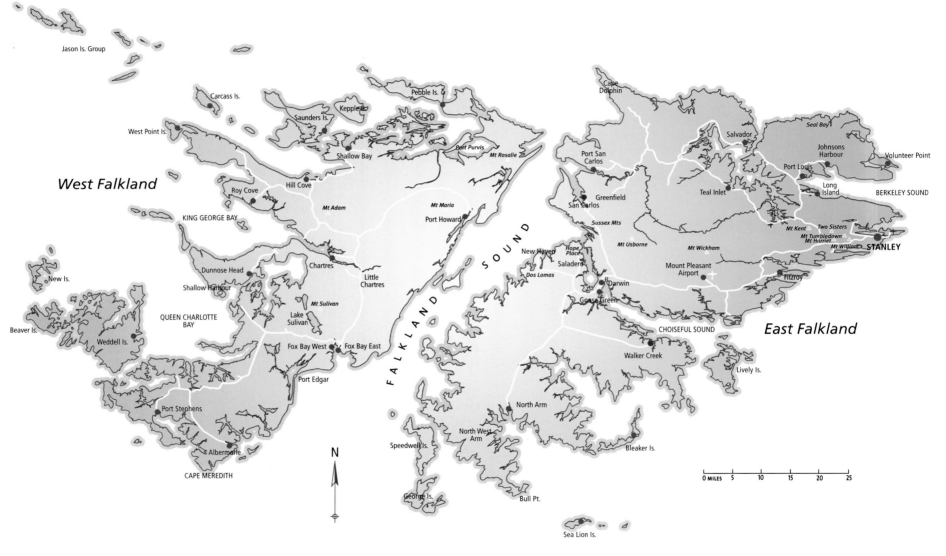

FALKLAND ISLANDS

Jason Is. Group

Carcass Is.

West Point Is.

Kepple Is.

Saunders Is.

Pebble Is.

Cape Dolphin

Port Purvis

Mt Rosalie

Shallow Bay

Salvador

Seal Bay

Johnsons Harbour

Volunteer Point

West Falkland

Roy Cove

Hill Cove

Port San Carlos

Port Louis

Long Island

BERKELEY SOUND

Mt Adam

Mt Maria

Teal Inlet

KING GEORGE BAY

Greenfield

San Carlos

Port Howard

Sussex Mts

Mt Kent

Two Sisters

Mt Tumbledown

Dunnose Head

Chartres

Mt Usborne

Mt Wickham

Mt Harriet

Mt William

STANLEY

New Is.

Shallow Harbour

Little Chartres

New Haven

Hope Place

Saladero

Mount Pleasant Airport

Beaver Is.

QUEEN CHARLOTTE BAY

Mt Sulivan

Dos Lomas

Fitzroy

Weddell Is.

Lake Sulivan

Darwin

Fox Bay West

Fox Bay East

Goose Green

CHOISEFUL SOUND

East Falkland

Port Edgar

Walker Creek

Lively Is.

Port Stephens

F
A
L
K
L
A
N
D

S
O
U
N
D

North Arm

North West Arm

Albermarle

Speedwell Is.

Bleaker Is.

CAPE MEREDITH

N

George Is.

Bull Pt.

0 MILES 5 10 15 20 25

Sea Lion Is.

Foreword

Twenty five years ago the Falkland Islands were a quiet and isolated corner of the globe. Today, their anonymity may be a thing of the past but, thankfully, they have remained unspoilt.

This new book, "Natural Ingredients, Taste of the Falklands", seeks to bring to a wider audience an essence of the unspoilt character of the South Atlantic. These recipes take the natural products of the islands, and the seas which surround them, and blend them into dishes full of the fresh flavours of the Falklands. They reflect the quality of the local produce and give the reader a sense of the warmth of the people.

Though we may not all be fortunate enough to visit these very special islands, I hope that through these pages, we gain a greater appreciation of their unique beauty and the rich variety of all they have to offer.

Margaret Thatcher

Baroness Margaret Thatcher
May 2007

FALKLAND
ISLANDS

I have great pleasure in introducing this superb new book 'Natural Ingredients: Taste of the Falklands'.

I came to the Falklands from the Caribbean, where the cuisine is suitably tropical, the sauces are spicy and the cocktails have hidden punch. I did not expect to find in the Falklands as exciting a cuisine as I have done. I have been agreeably surprised: this book shows what variety the Falkland Islands enjoy.

This book brings to us a taste of the Falklands as it is today, developed, vibrant and forward-thinking. The imagery and recipes not only will provide you with a mixture of tasty, stylish and practical dishes using the best Falklands ingredients, but also give you the chance to explore and discover the Falklands.

The book has been very carefully and creatively put together by Julie and Alex, I'm sure it is the beginning of a lot more to come. It is certainly one for all to share and enjoy; it is as much a coffee table book as a recipe collection and it is a magnificent example of the modern Falklands we live in today.

Alan Huckle
Governor of the Falkland Islands
May 2007

FALKLAND
ISLANDS

Introduction

We are a small nation living in a generous land of unspoilt beauty and abundant natural resources both on the land and in the sea. We are a people with a history of epic pioneering and a free-spirited way of life.

Natural Ingredients – Taste of the Falklands shows you some of the quality products we are able to enjoy locally. Green, clean and fresh ingredients like beef, lamb, goose, fish, shellfish, wild berries and dairy products have been used with enthusiasm and creativity to present you with an innovative selection of recipes in a modern and relaxed style of cooking.

Our dramatic landscape needs to be experienced first hand, and we hope this photographic showcase may inspire adventures of your own and bring you closer to the different scenic views we have to offer, the beauty of our rural landscape, the wildlife, our town, our people and the small things that make our country unique.

In the pages of this book you will see a pictorial combination of the freshest quality ingredients and the many different scenic delights of the Falklands. Enjoy the view – and your food.

View of the six hills and Purvis Harbour in the distance. (Next page)

FALKLAND ISLANDS

Mark of Origin

Falkland Islanders are proud of their beautiful home and the exceptional quality of goods produced in the Islands. Wool, meat, fish and handicrafts are among the many items produced in this stunning archipelago.

To identify home-grown goods, we use the Falkland Islands Mark of Origin. It shows the leaves of our native tussac grass waving freely in the South Atlantic wind.

The breezes that sweep across the tussac leaves as they grow on our coastlines bring a fresh, unpolluted air to everything that grows here. Meat and fish have a vital, wholesome flavour. Soft, warm wool is grown without chemicals on isolated farmsteads, and rich, sweet jams are made from wild local berries known as diddle-dee – and they all bear the Falkland Islands Mark of Origin.

Just like the tussac grass, products bearing the Mark of Origin embody the spirit of the Falklands – pristine, natural and completely unspoilt.

The productive seas in and around the Falklands provide an ideal fishing ground.
Below, snow crab.

Jigging arm and lure on a squid boat. (Right)

Fishing revenue is the most important contributor to the local economy.
A Falklands registered fishing vessel heading out to sea. (Below)

At fisheries licensing time, there can be anywhere up to 30 squid jiggers in Stanley harbour. (Bottom)

Calamari Patagonica

Ingredients

1kg clean squid tubes (Loligo gahi)

FILLING

500g crab meat
500g white breadcrumbs
200ml fresh cream
2 whole eggs, beaten
50ml extra virgin olive oil
100g red onion, chopped
2 cloves garlic, chopped
salt and freshly ground white pepper
pinch of nutmeg
extra virgin olive oil for grilling

SAUCE

400g chopped tomatoes
100ml extra virgin olive oil
100g onion, chopped
2 cloves garlic, minced
2 tablespoons chopped fresh basil
100ml white wine
1 teaspoon sugar
salt and pepper

Method

Fry garlic and onion in olive oil until soft but without adding colour, allow to cool. In a mixing bowl combine all remaining ingredients for the filling and add the onion mixture. Stuff the squid tubes with the crab filling and secure with a cocktail stick.

For the tomato sauce, fry onion and garlic in olive oil, add all other ingredients and simmer for 15 minutes, check seasoning.

Bring water to the boil in a large saucepan, add one teaspoon of salt and reduce heat. Carefully introduce the stuffed squid tubes into the water and simmer for 5 minutes; remove with a slotted spoon and drain well. Place on a lightly oiled tray and keep warm.

Heat cast iron pan and add some olive oil; seal the stuffed squid, place onto serving dish and pour on sauce. Serve with scattered basil leaves and dash of extra virgin olive oil.

FALKLAND
ISLANDS

Lamb Loin Wellington

Ingredients

2 boneless lamb loins
olive oil
salt and pepper
200g goose pate
500g filo pastry sheets

FOR THE DUXELLE

400g mushrooms, chopped
200g onion, chopped
50g butter
chopped parsley
hint of garlic
pinch of nutmeg
salt and pepper

Method

Heat the oil using a heavy based sauté pan, seal the loins and season with salt and pepper, remove from the pan and let stand over a wire rack.

Place the onions, mushrooms and butter into the same sauté pan, sweat over a gentle heat. Once cooked remove from the heat, add the parsley, seasonings and spices. Place into a covered container and refrigerate.

Spread goose pate over top of the lamb loins and cut into 6 equal pieces. Spoon on top an amount of duxelle and wrap loins neatly in pastry with the seal underneath the loin, allow to rest.

Brush with egg-wash and bake in hot oven until golden brown and cooked. Serve with roast potatoes, steamed vegetables and Madeira sauce (see page 110).

Judges look on as Critta Lee competes during the annual sports week holiday shearing competition on West Falklands. (Above)

Lambs arriving at the Falkland Islands Meat Company. (Left)

Bill Shaw, thought to have shorn over two million sheep, pulls another roughie onto the shearing floor. (Facing)

FALKLAND ISLANDS

Above, the garden of Cartmell Cottage, one of Stanley's first homes, built in 1849. Locally produced felted designs by Fiona Didlick. (Above right)

Mussels with Spaghetti and Gremolata

Ingredients

120ml dry white wine
½ cup chicken stock
4 spring onions, chopped
1 red pepper, seeded and chopped
2kg mussels, scrubbed and bearded
500g cooked spaghetti

GREMOLATA

2 tablespoons chopped fresh coriander
2 tablespoons chopped fresh basil
2 cloves garlic, chopped
juice and rind of 1 lemon
100ml extra virgin olive oil
salt and freshly ground black pepper

Method

For the gremolata, combine all the ingredients and season to taste.

Combine wine, chicken stock, red pepper and spring onions in a large saucepan and simmer until reduced by half. Add mussels, cover and cook until the mussels open (discard any unopened), incorporate the pasta, stir and cover to heat through. Transfer mussels and pasta to warm pasta bowls and pour over a generous amount of gremolata, serve immediately with crusty bread.

The Canache is a popular place for yachts to moor.
The backdrop shows Stanley and the Two Sisters covered in snow.

Upland Goose Casserole

Ingredients

6 goose legs
seasoned flour
50ml vegetable oil
1 onion, large diced
200g carrots, thick sliced
2 leeks, cut in four
2 bay leaves
6 cloves
1kg green apples, cored and quartered
1 can cider
500ml chicken stock
salt and pepper

Method

Coat goose legs with seasoned flour. Heat the oil using a large casserole pan, seal the goose legs until brown. Remove meat from the pan, add onion, carrots, leeks, bay leaves, cloves and green apples. Fry quickly, add cider and stock, season to taste. Return goose legs to the pot, cover and cook in a hot oven for 1½ hours. Serve with potato and turnip mash.

Councillor, Mike Rendell trying to conquer the mechanical bull; Children dressed in hand-made woollen garments from the Falklands Wool Centre playing in the Surf Bay dunes. (Top)

Parents and children gather as HRH Prince Andrew opens the Infant and Junior School extension. (Above)

The Stanley Races occur every year between Christmas and New Year. A horse and rider version of musical chairs. (Left)

FALKLAND ISLANDS

Lambs brought into the Falkland Island Meat Company abattoir. (Below)

Paddocks at the old meat works in West Stanley. (Bottom)

Lamb Casserole with Seasonal Vegetables

Ingredients

800g boned lamb, large diced
50ml olive oil
1 onion, large diced
hint of garlic
30g flour
500ml meat stock

200g baby carrots
200g baby leeks
200g sliced green and yellow courgettes
6 spring onions, chopped
salt and pepper
fresh thyme

Method: Lightly season meat with salt and pepper, seal quickly in heated oil until brown. Remove meat from the pan and sweat onions with garlic until soft, add the flour and form a pale roux (see page 111), stir in the stock, bring to the boil and skim. Return meat to the pan and add the vegetables, cover with lid and braise steadily in a moderately hot oven until meat is cooked. Serve with garlic mashed potatoes and steamed broccoli.

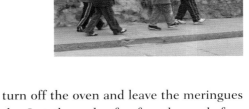

Meringue Wafers with Summer Fruit Cream

Ingredients

1 x quantity Italian meringue (see page 73)
450g mixed red fruits
zest of 1 orange and 1 lemon
50g caster sugar
25ml Grand Marnier
600ml double cream

Method

Preheat the oven to 140°C. Cut out two pieces of parchment paper large enough to line two baking sheets. With a tablespoon place mounds of meringue and spread into circles, bake for 1 hour, turn off the oven and leave the meringues to cool. Let them dry for four hours before using them.

Mash the fruit with the sugar, lightly whisk the cream and fold in the liqueur, then fold in the mashed fruit.

Sandwich the meringue wafers with the summer fruit cream and decorate with some fresh berries.

World War I Monument, commemorating the defeat of the German Navy by the British, at the Battle of the Falklands, December 8, 1914. (Left)

The last stage of the 74-day Falklands War when Argentina invaded the Falklands was the liberation of Stanley on June 14th, 1982.
"Liberation Day" is commemorated annually by members of the British Armed Forces and Falkland Islands Defence Force,
as well as other local organisations. The majority of the community attend this event. (Below)
The centre wall detail of the bronze relief on the 1982 Memorial in Stanley. (Below right)

The 20 foot high polished granite memorial (bottom) was created inscribed with the names of the units that took part in the campaign.

Crab Cakes

Ingredients

500g crab meat, well drained
2 spring onions, chopped
1 tablespoon chives, chopped
250g fresh wholemeal breadcrumbs
dash fish sauce
1 tablespoon cocktail sauce
tabasco sauce, few drops to taste
1 whole egg, beaten
oil for frying

Method

Mix all ingredients, binding with the egg. Refrigerate to set. Divide the mixture into 8 portions and shape into a medallion on a lightly floured board. Shallow fry steadily in oil on both sides until cooked. Drain and serve with green salad and tartare sauce.

One of the first things cruise ship visitors will see in Stanley is the southernmost cathedral in the world, Christ Church Cathedral consecrated in 1892. Alongside is whalebone arch, raised in 1933. (Facing)

A Royal Airforce and Fleet Air Arm helicopter are displayed on the Stanley Community School field for the pupils to visit. (Below)

The colourful new housing development in East Stanley. (Facing)

A mixture of old and new with typical Falklands' cottages and more modern housing. (Right and below)

First lit on December 1st 1855, the Cape Pembroke Lighthouse is just seven miles due east of Stanley on the most easterly point of the Falklands. (Below)

Government House, the home of the Falkland Islands' London-appointed Governors, since the mid-19th century. (Facing below)

FALKLAND
ISLANDS

Berrying time in the Falklands is in autumn, time to collect wild berries such as diddle-dee or teaberries.
Mountain berries. (Right)

The Pale Maiden is the national flower of the Falkland Islands. (Far right)

One of the best preserved shipwrecks, the Jhelum in West Stanley was built in Liverpool in 1849 and condemned in Stanley in 1870. (Below)

Teaberry and Raspberry Crème Brulée

Ingredients

600ml double cream
80g caster sugar
½ teaspoon vanilla essence
5 egg yolks
100g raspberries
100g teaberries
extra sugar to glaze

Method

Preheat the oven to 140°C. Put the cream in a saucepan and gently bring to the boil. In a bowl mix the sugar, vanilla essence and egg yolks. Incorporate the hot cream and pass through a sieve. Sprinkle some sugar over the raspberries and teaberries and divide into 6 small ramekin dishes, pour the custard in and transfer to a deep baking tray, add enough cold water to cover half of the outside of the ramekin dishes, then cook in the oven for 1 hour. Remove from the oven and transfer the ramekins to a wire rack, refrigerate until cold. Sprinkle 1 teaspoon of sugar over the top of each brulée and caramelise with a blowtorch.

Based at Mullet Creek, Stanley Dairy supplies the community with fresh milk, cream, eggs, cheese, other dairy products and even milk soap.

FALKLAND ISLANDS

Smoked Mullet with Vegetable Rosti and Hollandaise Sauce

Ingredients

2 fresh mullet fillets
1 hot smoker/wok
100g each grated, potatoes, carrots, turnip
  & swedes
1 teaspoon minced garlic
vegetable oil for frying
1 tablespoon cornflour
seasoning

FOR THE HOLLANDAISE SAUCE

500g butter
6 whole black peppercorns
25ml tarragon wine vinegar
3 egg yolks

Method

For the rosti, mix all ingredients in a bowl and season with salt and pepper, shape into cakes using a metal ring, pan-fry on both sides and transfer to a medium hot oven for 15 minutes.

Using a hot smoker or a wok, smoke the fillet of mullet for about ten minutes – the fish must be tender and moist.

For the sauce, melt the butter gently. In a saucepan reduce vinegar by half with the peppercorns. Using a food processor, whisk the egg yolks and incorporate the cooled reduced vinegar, then incorporate the butter until sauce forms.

To serve, arrange the fish on top of the rosti and pour over some hollandaise sauce.

John-Maskell Bott's winning recipe from the Natural Ingredients – Taste of the Falklands cooking competition with participation from the community.

Daffodills pop-up in spring and when bulbs are imported from the northern hemisphere, occasionally in autumn too. Surf Bay changes dramatically during the winter months; Boulder landscape. (Above)

FALKLAND
ISLANDS

Strong wind blowing off the surf at Surf Bay. (Facing)

Sunning its bald red face, the non-aggressive turkey vulture can be found roosting in large community groups or breaking away to forage independently during the day; Mine fields are scattered over the Falklands as a reminder of the 1982 conflict. (Bottom right)

52° South Ceviche

Ingredients

400g smoked mullet
200g squid cut into rings
200g scallops
1kg freshly poached mussels, discard the shells
100ml white wine
juice of 4 lemons
1 onion, chopped
1 tablespoon chopped parsley
1 green pepper, chopped
1 small red chilli, chopped
50ml olive oil
salt and pepper

Method

Place together into a saucepan the diced smoked mullet, squid rings and scallops, add the white wine and some of the lemon juice. Gently simmer for 3 minutes, leave to cool and drain all the liquid. Transfer into a glass bowl and add the mussels, onion, parsley, pepper, red chilli, olive oil and seasoning. Marinade for 15 minutes in the refrigerator and serve in wide opening glasses with halved garnish with thinly sliced mixed peppers.

FALKLAND ISLANDS

Calamari & Scallops Etouffée

Ingredients

300g squid cut into rings
300g scallops
450g chopped tomatoes
1 onion, chopped
1 clove garlic, chopped
1 red pepper, chopped
½ cup chopped celery
100ml olive oil
1 tablespoon flour
100ml white wine
good pinch cayenne pepper
1 tablespoon dried basil
salt and pepper

Method

Heat the oil in a sauté pan, fry the onions with the garlic until soft. Add the chopped red pepper and the celery and fry gently. Add the flour and cook until golden brown, add the chopped tomatoes and the wine, simmer for 10 minutes then add the cayenne pepper, dried basil, salt and pepper. Stir in the squid rings and scallops and sauté for 4 to 6 minutes, check seasoning and serve immediately. This dish can be served with boiled white rice as a main meal.

The bow from the 'Charles Cooper', a 1855 Connecticut packet ship. (Far left)

Rock shags can be found on steep cliffs, ship wrecks or jetties (middle)

A male Long-tailed meadow lark, commonly known as the "Military Starling" because of its red breast. (Left)

Delicate early morning frosted carpet of fern. (Above)

Abandoned fuel drums. (Top left)

FALKLAND
ISLANDS

Kingclip with Herb Crust

Ingredients

4 kingclip fillets
dijon mustard
olive oil
sea salt and freshly ground black pepper

HERB CRUST

200g fresh white breadcrumbs
1 cup chopped mixed herbs (basil, parsley,
  tarragon, chives, oregano)
zest and juice of 1 lemon
1 teaspoon crushed pink peppercorns
1 tablespoon green peppercorns in brine, drained
50g melted butter

Method

To make the crust, combine all the ingredients in a glass bowl, mixing thoroughly using a fork.

Place the fish fillets onto an oiled baking sheet, brush each fillet with a thin layer of Dijon mustard and season with a little salt and pepper. Coat the fish with the herb crust and drizzle with some olive oil. Bake in a hot oven for 10 to 15 minutes. Discard the juices and serve with sautéed vegetables.

Looking west up the track towards the 'Two Sisters'

Smoked Trout or Smoked Upland Goose Tartare

Ingredients

1 side smoked trout, skinless
2 hard-boiled eggs, chopped
1 medium size onion, chopped
100g capers
2 carrots, grated
mustard seeds
2 tablespoons chopped parsley

DRESSING

2 tablespoons Dijon mustard
100ml olive oil
100ml tarragon white wine vinegar
salt and pepper

buttered granary bread

Method

Cut smoked trout into 2cm thick strips, or if using smoked upland goose, slice thinly. Mix grated carrots with mustard seeds and chopped parsley. To make the dressing, mix all ingredients with a small whisk and season to taste.

Place trout and all other ingredients into service platter with little mounds of hard-boiled eggs, capers, onions and carrots. Pour some dressing on top and serve with the granary bread.

Low cloud rolls over Smoko Mountain. (Facing) Fishing is a favoured pastime in the Falklands. Mullet, trout, and smelt are caught in the small creeks around the Islands, sometimes with a net or with a line. Fitzroy River, a popular fishing spot. (Above)

The unusual suede-like sea cabbage can be found on the sandy shores, while the pretty Falklands lavender can be found over hanging cliffs or in the low lying scrubs. (Above) Whitegrass covers most of the Falklands. (Below)

This fence provides a barrier to sheep and cattle from crossing at low tide. (Facing)

The road between Stanley and Mount Pleasant Airport (MPA) is 35 miles, mostly unsealed. (Top)

Balsam bog creeps up and over a boulder field in one of the many Falklands' stone runs. Looking south east from Mount Kent road. (Left)

Eerie clouds crawl the Wickham Heights. (Above left)

Looking west from Mount Harriet towards Mount Pleasant. (Above right)

Aerial view of the road between Mount Pleasant Airport and Stanley. (Facing)

Toothfish and Scallops en Papillote

Ingredients

800g toothfish fillet boned and skinned
  cut into six pieces
300g scallops
6 tablespoons white wine
6 teaspoons fish sauce
grated ginger
300g sliced carrots, cooked
1 onion, sliced
1 yellow pepper, cut into rings
1 lemon, cut into slices
30 small potato dumplings (see page 110)
olive oil for brushing
6 large sheets tin foil

Method

Heat oven. Brush oil over centre of tin foil,
place one piece of fish on centre of each piece
of foil; arrange carrots, onion, yellow pepper,
scallops and lemon over the fish. Sprinkle
grated ginger on top, pour wine and fish sauce,
season with some black pepper and arrange five
potato dumplings around the edge of the fish.

Fold up each end of the paper and securely
seal. Bake in hot oven for 15 to 20 minutes.
Place foil packets on serving plate and open
from centre with a pair of scissors.

North camp and Estancia come into view. (Below)

Detail of the boulders from a stone run, thought to be caused by the most recent ice age. (Bottom right)

This view from Mount Harriet shows Stanley and Mount William in the distance. (Above)

A crisp morning from the top of Mount Pleasant. (Left)

There are a few corrals around the Falklands. They were, and some still are, used to contain horses or cattle. The corrals are made of stone or wood and designed in a circle. The stone corral outside Stanley. (Far left)

FALKLAND
ISLANDS

Toothfish Brochettes

Ingredients

1kg toothfish loins, cut into very large cubes
1 onion, large diced
12 lemon wedges
12 bamboo skewers
sea salt and cracked black pepper

FOR THE MARINADE

50ml olive oil
juice of two lemons
1 tablespoon chopped tarragon
1 tablespoon chopped basil
1 tablespoon chopped chives
1 teaspoon sugar
salt and pepper

FOR THE PEPERONATA

2 tablespoons olive oil
2 garlic cloves, chopped
1 each roast red, green and yellow pepper
 thinly sliced
salt and pepper

Method

To prepare the brochettes, skewer the fish with the large diced onion and finish with lemon wedge, lightly season with salt and pepper. Combine all marinade ingredients with a whisk and pour over the fish. Cook under a hot grill.

To prepare the peperonata heat the oil in a frying pan and fry the garlic for a few seconds, add the roast peppers, season and mix thoroughly. Serve with polenta cakes (see page 110) and green salad.

FALKLAND ISLANDS

The water tank at Johnsons Harbour. (Above)

A camp bogging with a storm on the horizon. To "get bogged" usually means a vehicle or animal has become stuck in the mud, in a ditch or other boggy place. (Right)

This view of Volunteer beach is enjoyed by thousands of penguins every year. (Top)

The friendly and curious king penguins. (Above)

The intricate bronze cast sculptures of taxidermist and artist, Steve Massam, who works at the Falklands museum. (Above right)

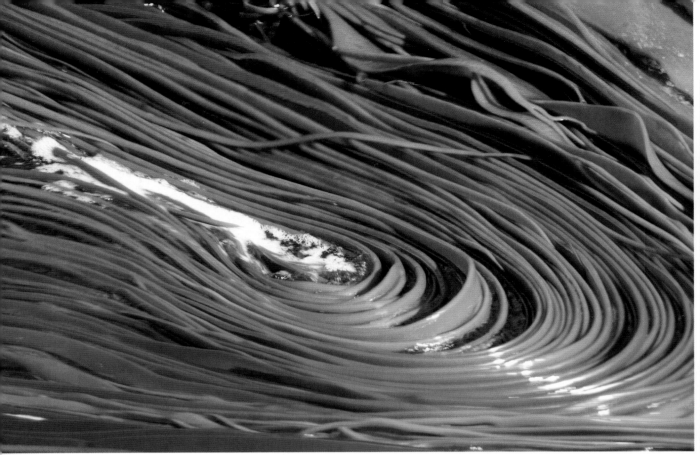

The coast of the Falklands is filled with large streamers of broad-leafed kelp, an ideal resting place for many seabirds. The kelp is often broken up by winter storms and piled on the beaches. (Above)

Found at Cape Dolphin a large male sealion and his harem in the tussac grass. (Right top)
Driving through Swan Pond to Seal Bay. (Above right)

Scurvy grass, a widely distributed, arctic cress reputed to have been valued by sailors to prevent the onset of scurvy; Blackish oyster catcher's nest; Moulting Magellanic penguins. (Left)

Flock of upland geese. (Facing)

FALKLAND
ISLANDS

Upland Goose Terrine

Ingredients

1 large goose
200g chicken breast, cut into pieces
150g chicken livers
150g gammon, cut into pieces
150g bacon rashers
50g onion, chopped
1 whole egg
100ml cream

100g white breadcrumbs
50g butter

SEASONING

1 orange, zest and juice
1 clove garlic, chopped
50ml brandy
pinch thyme, marjoram, nutmeg, allspice,
salt and pepper to taste

Method

Bone the goose removing any skin and sinew. Cut into pieces and place into a container with the gammon, chicken breast and chicken liver. Melt the butter in a saucepan, fry the chopped onions with the garlic and sweat under cover to soften without colour, allow to cool. Place on top of the forcemeat mixture. Mix cream with the egg and pour over the forcemeat and fried onion, add seasoning, liquor and orange juice and zest. Cover with cling film and marinade for at least two hours.

Mix all ingredients by hand and pass through food processor. Line terrine dish with the bacon rashers and fill with the forcemeat, then fold over the bacon rashers to fully enclose. Cover the terrine with a lid and cook in a bain marie for 1hr. Once cooked, remove from oven and discard all juices, wrap in cling film and store in the fridge until cold and set. Cut into medium size slices and serve with crusty bread, butter and diddle-dee preserve (See page 112).

FALKLAND ISLANDS

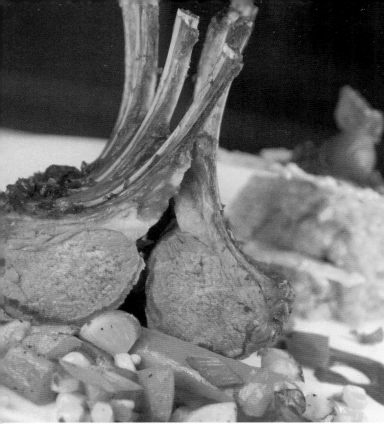

Rack of Lamb au Chocolat

Ingredients

2 racks of lamb
4 cloves garlic, chopped
salt and pepper
2 tablespoons coriander seeds
1 teaspoon ground cumin

juice and rind of 1 lemon
60ml olive oil
250ml demi-glace sauce
50g plain chocolate
pinch of dried red chillies

Method

Pre-heat oven to very hot. Blend garlic, coriander seeds, ground cumin, juice and lemon rind and olive oil until mixture forms into a paste. Cut slits between cutlets with sharp knife and push a little of the paste into each slit, press remaining paste over outside of racks. Roast in very hot oven for about 35 minutes.

Heat demi-glace sauce and add the chocolate broken into pieces, add the dried red chillies and stir until all the chocolate has melted. Serve with pumpkin risotto (see page 111) and steamed vegetables.

Cattle/sheep pen. (Left)

This sandstone contains a fossil of a trilobite. (Below)

Falklands green spider typically lives in the gorse. (Right)

Turf walls and corrals were commonly constructed in the early days of a settlement to give shelter around a garden. Gorse hedges were often planted on top. (Right)

Port San Carlos settlement. (Facing)

Lamb Shanks Puchero

Ingredients

6 lamb shanks
100ml olive oil
1kg pumpkin, cut into chunks
1kg potatoes, peeled and cut in half
3 whole leeks, cut in half
500g carrots, cut into large chunks
1lt lamb stock
2 onions, large diced
oregano
2 red peppers, seeded and quartered
2 sprigs rosemary
salt and pepper
3 corn on the cob, cut into three pieces
500g loose cabbage leaves
500g chick peas, soaked overnight

Method

Heat the oil in a large and deep saucepan, season and seal the shanks until brown, add the vegetables to the pan and sweat for 5 minutes with the lid on. Add the oregano and rosemary and gradually incorporate the stock and the soaked chick peas, season with salt and pepper and place the loose cabbage leaves on top. Cook for an hour on medium heat until the stock has evaporated and the meat is tender, the stock will thicken with the starch from the potatoes. Perfect for a cold winter's day.

Once the sole means of heating and cooking and the core of the house, a typical Rayburn peat stove. (Above)

A curious red backed hawk. (Below)

Cutting the peat into sods (peat blocks) is usually done in the early spring. Traditionally cut by hand, it is now more often machine cut. The peat then dries on the bank and is carted to the peat stack in late summer. An average household would burn roughly 120-140 sq. yards of peat in one year. Laguna Isla peat bog. (Below)

Camp is a popular weekend destination for Islanders. Fun at sunset, a game of rounders; Getting close with part of a drying stack of peat, a rickling. (Facing)

Looking down to Head of the Bay, San Carlos and Ajax Bay. (Above)

Originally a refrigeration plant, the buildings at Ajax Bay were used as a military hospital during the Falklands War. (Facing top)
San Carlos cemetery. (Facing middle top) Mint often found around settlements. (Facing top right) Ajax Bay. (Facing bottom)

Tarte Tatin

Ingredients
8 green apples, cored, peeled and halved
200g caster sugar
150g unsalted butter
pinch cinnamon
300g puff pastry
egg wash

Method
Using an oven-proof frying pan with high sides, melt the butter with the sugar and pinch of cinnamon, pack the apples in as tightly as possible. Cook on top of the stove for about 40 minutes on low heat until caramelised.

Roll out the puff pastry and prick with a fork, place on top of the apples and cut the excess pastry. Egg wash and bake in the oven until golden brown. Turn over onto a serving dish, serve with vanilla icecream and fresh cream.

FALKLAND
ISLANDS

Grilled Kingclip, Bean and Chorizo Stew

Ingredients

4 kingclip fillets, skinned
1 garlic clove, chopped
sea salt and pepper
juice of 1 lemon
olive oil
500g dried beans, soaked and cooked

1 onion, chopped
100g chorizo, thinly sliced and grilled
1 cup mixed peppers, chopped
pinch of dried red chillies
1 cup short grain rice
½ cup sweetcorn
1lt vegetable stock

Method

Season fish fillets with salt and pepper, sprinkle chopped garlic and lemon juice over the fish and drizzle a small amount of olive oil; refrigerate until ready to cook using a very hot cast iron frying pan.

Fry onion and peppers in hot oil, add the beans, chorizo and pinch of dried chillies, add vegetable stock, bring to the boil and add the rice and sweetcorn, simmer gently until almost all the liquid is absorbed and the rice is cooked. Serve in pasta bowl with the fish placed on top.

Goose Green settlement. (Above)

2 Para memorial at Darwin; Bodie Creek bridge at Goose Green,
the most southerly suspension bridge in the world; and the Galpon (shed),
Darwin settlement. (Left)

Looking east from the standing man (a marker built for travellers) at
Hill Head. (Facing)

FALKLAND
ISLANDS

An easterly view from Sussex Mountains. (Below)

Dramatic double rainbow near Swan Inlet. (Bottom left)

Looking towards Sussex Mountains (Bottom middle)

Swan Inlet River. (Bottom right)

Mount Usborne, the highest mountain in the Falklands. (Facing)

Hope Place, established as a salting plant in 1847 for Samuel Fisher Lafone. (Above)

Magellanic oystercatchers. (Left)

An old roll of fencing wire is left behind. (Facing)

FALKLAND
ISLANDS

Seafood Canneloni/Pancakes

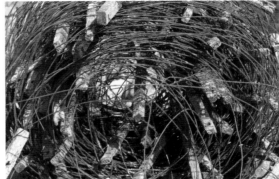

Ingredients

500g fresh mullet fillets, cut into cubes
200g poached and shelled mussels
250g crab meat
1 onion, chopped
chopped fresh parsley
½ cup white wine
salt and pepper
100g butter

100g flour
1lt milk
100g grated Cheddar cheese
500g basic tomato sauce
1 teaspoon sugar
1 dozen lasagne sheets, blanched
  or 1 dozen pancakes

Method

Place mullet onto ovenproof dish with the onion, wine and milk, poach for 5 minutes, drain and reserve the liquid.

Melt the butter and form a white roux (see page 111) using the flour. Gradually add the heated milk to the roux stirring thoroughly and continuously to the boil. Season with salt and pepper. Reserve half of the sauce. Place the remaining sauce into a large mixing bowl, add the poached fish, mussels, crab meat and parsley.

Place the soft lasagne sheets over a damp tea towel and spoon a generous amount of the fish filling at one end of the pasta sheet, then roll.

Add the sugar to the tomato sauce and spread over an oven proof dish, place the cannelloni on top and coat with the remaining white sauce, sprinkle the grated Cheddar cheese and bake for 40 minutes in a hot oven.

Coconut Crème Caramel

Ingredients

CARAMEL
115g caster sugar
50ml water plus 1 tablespoon water

CUSTARD CREAM
250ml fresh full fat cream
250ml coconut milk
140ml double cream
4 whole eggs
2 egg yolks
45g caster sugar
seeds of 1 vanilla pod
50g desiccated coconut

Method

For the caramel, pour water and sugar into a saucepan. Boil rapidly until golden brown, do not stir. Remove from the heat and carefully add

the tablespoon of water, pour caramel into the moulds to cover the base.

For the custard, whisk together the whole eggs, egg yolks and sugar. Scrape the seeds from the vanilla pod into a saucepan with the milk. Heat slowly, then stir into the egg mixture, pass through a sieve and add the desiccated coconut. Pour the custard into moulds and bake in bain-marie at 170°C for 15-20 minutes. When cool refrigerate until required. Turn out onto serving dish with extra cream and toasted coconut.

Kelp Creek stone corral (Facing).

Along the track to Wreck House, North Arm. (Above)

Dos Lomas kitchen window; Typical "wriggly" tin of the Fanny Cove house; and campers dance at North Arm club, which proudly shows the British and Falklands flags. Most youngsters learn the traditional dances of foxtrot, quick step and samba at a young age. (Left)

Dos Lomas shanty, long drop and shed, looking towards snow capped West Falklands. (Below)

Rueben Harwood demonstrating how the hand shears are used. (Right)

Most houses in the West and outer Islands use generators to provide their electrical power. Using wind turbines to collect the Falklands' naturally strong winds provides additional power. (Right top)

Regular shipping between the Islands and Stanley links the East with the West. (Below)

Snow-capped Mount Maria provides a scenic backdrop to Port Howard settlement. (Facing)

Myles Lee filling the pens with sheep in preparation for shearing. (Left)

A sheepdog patiently waits to be called in; Les Morrison lamb marking. (Below)

Driving the sheep on Port Howard farm. (Bottom)

Tin dog, used to rattle the sheep! (Below)

Stuffed Shoulder of Lamb

Ingredients

2 boneless lamb shoulders
300g scallops
baby chard leaves
2 garlic cloves, pureed
salt and pepper
100ml olive oil
1 onion, diced
200g chopped carrots
2 bay leaves
2 sprigs fresh rosemary
2 cans dry cider
6 whole black peppercorns
string

Method

Season the lamb shoulders with salt and pepper, rub the garlic puree over them, arrange the baby chard leaves onto the meat and top with the scallops, roll and secure with the string.

Heat the oil in a heavy based braising pan and seal the meat rolls until brown. Remove from the pan and add the onions and carrots, cook over high heat for a few minutes until the onions are soft, add the bay leaves, rosemary and peppercorns. Place the rolled meat on top of the vegetables and pour over the cider, season with more salt and pepper, cover with lid and braise in a hot oven for 1 hour, leave to rest before cutting into thick slices. Serve with the pan sauce, rosti potatoes and seasonal vegetables.

FALKLAND
ISLANDS

Smoked Mullet

Frittata

Ingredients

8 fresh eggs
100g fresh ricotta cheese, lightly beaten
  with a fork
200g smoked mullet, sliced
2 teaspoons chopped fresh marjoram
50g Parmesan cheese, freshly grated
salt and freshly ground black pepper
2 tablespoons olive oil

Method

Pre-heat the oven to 200°C

Break the eggs into a bowl and beat lightly. Add 75g of the ricotta, reserving the rest, together with most of the marjoram, most of the Parmesan, and salt and pepper to taste. Stir to combine.

In a small ovenproof frying pan, heat the olive oil, tilting the pan to coat all sides. Add the egg mixture and lower the heat. Cook over a low heat, loosening the eggs at the sides from time to time, until just set.

Scatter with the rest of the marjoram, ricotta and smoked mullet, and place in the hot oven for a few seconds only. Loosen the frittata from the pan with a long spatula and put onto a warm plate. Scatter over the remaining Parmesan and cut into wedges to serve.

The road out of Port Howard was constructed around this hawks nest encouraging the breeding hawks to return year after year. (Top)

Lamb marking; the ewes with their lambs are gathered, they are counted, their tails are docked, the males are castrated and the ears are marked to indicate the age, sex and origin. (Above)

FALKLAND
ISLANDS

Pasture improvement at Port Howard. (Facing)

Crab and Smoked Trout Ravioli

Ingredients

FILLING

500g crab meat
500g smoked trout, flaked
200g fresh breadcrumbs
200g ricotta cheese, well drained
2 egg yolks
dash of fish sauce
1cm grated ginger
2 tablespoons chives, chopped
2 tablespoons fresh cream
salt and pepper

FRESH EGG SPINACH PASTA

800g strong flour
4 eggs, beaten
salt to taste
100g spinach, cooked and puréed
semolina for dusting

SAUCE

200ml dry white wine
6 cloves garlic, sliced and roasted
50g butter
500ml fresh cream
pinch of chilli powder
salt and pepper

Method

Sift flour and salt, form a well. Pour egg into well, combine with flour to form a smooth and developed dough. Incorporate the spinach. Cover with damp cloth and rest in a cool place for at least 30 minutes before use.

In a bowl combine all the filling ingredients by hand, mix thoroughly, season to taste and refrigerate for 15 minutes.

Roll out pasta dough through pasta machine into a large paper-thin rectangle. Dust working surface with semolina and place filling in even spaced mounds, moisten edges with water using your fingers and cover with another strip of pastry, press down firmly and cut ravioli with pastry cutter, avoiding air pockets. Place on greaseproof paper dusted with semolina.

For the sauce, reduce white wine by half over high heat, add garlic, butter, cream, chilli powder and seasoning, gently simmer until sauce thickens. Keep warm.

Boil water in a large saucepan, add a good pinch of salt, simmer ravioli gently to 'al dente'. Drain well in colander, place in serving dish with extra virgin olive oil and freshly ground black pepper. Pour the sauce over it and serve with shavings of Parmesan cheese.

FALKLAND ISLANDS

Baked Alaska with Fudge Sauce

Ingredients

6 x 5cm diameter sponge discs (see page 111)
6 teaspoons strawberry jam
6 scoops vanilla ice cream
granulated sugar for dusting

ITALIAN MERINGUE

240g granulated sugar
120g egg whites
80ml water
pinch cream of tartare

FUDGE SAUCE

175g unsalted butter
175g dark soft brown sugar
150ml double cream
½ teaspoon vanilla essence

Method

Sprinkle sugar over a baking sheet and arrange sponge discs, spread strawberry jam over each disc and place scoop of ice cream, on top press down a little and put in the freezer.

The spectacular view from Mount Darcy and Green Hill looking over the track carved through the stone run.

For the Italian meringue, mix sugar, water and cream of tartare in boiling pan, bring to the boil and reduce by half. Whisk the egg whites to stiff peaks, gradually pour in a fine steady stream of the hot syrup to fully incorporate, and continue whisking until a light meringue is formed. Fill up a piping bag fitted with a large star nozzle and pipe the meringue over the ice cream to cover completely, place in the freezer.

For the fudge sauce, place all ingredients in a saucepan and gently bring to the boil until butter and sugar is fully dissolved.

In a very hot oven, bake the Alaskas for 3 minutes. Serve with the hot fudge sauce.

Purvis house – no longer occupied. (Top)

The remnants of the old peat stack and dog kennels.
Old iron pots highlights days gone by. (Left)

The view looking back towards Purvis Rincon along the
wonderful golden sandy beach. (Facing)

Sports week is an annual holiday held on the East and West Falklands consisting of sheepdog trials, horse racing, shearing competitions, foot events and topped off with plenty of dancing in the evenings. The air strip at Shallow Bay provides a great track for the horse racing. (Below)

Westers, Paul and Dae Peck preparing their horses to race. (Facing top)

Sheltering from a squall, outside the tote shed at the races, Ron Rozee, Tracy Pearce, Bella McKay, Chris Lloyd and Jeff Halliday. (Facing left)

In recent years the art of making horse gear has nearly disappeared from the Islands. Horse gear hand crafted by Paul Peck, saddle and leather artist, who works from a small workshop at Shallow Bay. (Bottom)

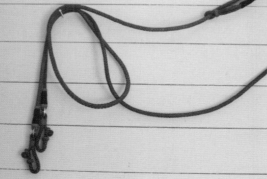

Teaberry Clafoutis

Ingredients

1kg ripe teaberries
50g brown sugar
2 tablespoons lemon juice
40ml brandy
110g plain flour, sifted
160g icing sugar, sifted
1½ cups milk
1 cup fresh cream
4 eggs
icing sugar for dusting

Method

Place teaberries, brown sugar, lemon juice and brandy in a saucepan, stir gently and place in a hot oven for 15 minutes, drain, reserve pan juices and cool teaberries at room temperature.

Using an electric mixer, combine flour and icing sugar. Mix milk, cream and half cup reserved pan juices. At slow speed, gradually incorporate milk mixture to dry ingredients and beat until smooth. Add one egg at a time, until batter is formed. Place teaberries in a well buttered shallow ceramic baking dish. Pour batter over and bake at 180°C for 50 minutes until the clafoutis is set and golden brown, dust with icing sugar and serve immediately with sweetened yoghurt.

FALKLAND ISLANDS

Steak & Lamb Kidney Pie

Ingredients

600g large diced beef
100g onion, finely diced
100g carrots, grated
300g lamb kidneys, cleaned and cut into
   large cubes
30g flour
30ml oil
1 tablespoon tomato purée
seasoning
1 garlic clove, chopped
1 can Guinness
brown stock
1kg short crust pastry

Method

Lightly season meat with salt and pepper and seal quickly in heated oil to colour light brown. Add onion, grated carrots and continue cooking, add flour and stir for a couple of minutes. Add tomato puree, seasoning, garlic and lamb kidneys, incorporate the Guinness and sufficient stock to cover the meat.

Cover with lid, stew gently on stove top, check periodically until meat is cooked. Once meat is cooked transfer into a clean heatproof dish and allow to cool down. Roll out pastry and line individual pie dishes, fill up with meat stew and cover with pastry lids, pierce a little hole in each pie and brush with some egg wash, oven bake. Serve with snow peas and home-made chips.

FALKLAND ISLANDS

Below, an asado barbeque, where meat is skewered on large metal stakes and cooked rotisserie style over burning wood embers.

Shearing in the Shallow Bay shed. (Below)

Picturesque Shallow Bay. (Facing)

Harold Neilson cooking up a storm at Hill Cove sports week; An old nissan hut, formerly known as "Dick's Bar". (Above)

Three Fish Platter

Ingredients

1 trout fillet
1 kingclip fillet
1 mero fillet
12 whole squid tubes, cleaned

MARINADE

¼ cup olive oil
1 teaspoon garlic paste
1 tablespoon chopped parsley
1 tablespoon chopped tarragon
1 teaspoon sugar
2 tablespoons balsamic vinegar
1 teaspoon wholegrain mustard
salt and pepper

Method

For the marinade, combine all ingredients in a glass bowl using a metal whisk. Divide fish into four pieces and marinade for 15 minutes, reserve 1 or 2 tablespoons of the marinade. Gently place on a well-oiled barbecue or cast iron frying pan and char-grill. Cook squid tubes last with the remaining marinade. Serve with creamed potatoes (see page 111), sour cream and chives.

Dandelions sprinkle the fields during the summer months. (Left)

Bella McKay's vegetable garden at Hill Cove and a leaning macrocarpa tree, typical in the Falklands with the prevailing westerly winds; Dogs eagerly wait to go gathering. (Below)

FALKLAND
ISLANDS

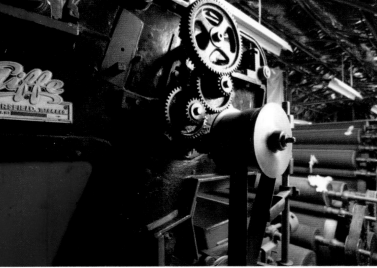

A spectacular early morning looking over Lakelands ponds. (Top)

Joyce Halliday's vegetable garden and tending to her many free-range chickens. The eggs are supplied to local shops. (Above)

The old wool carder at Fox Bay Mill. (Left)

Power lines going past the old doctor's house. (Facing)

FALKLAND ISLANDS

FALKLAND
ISLANDS

Beef Ajiaco

Ingredients
600g rump of beef cut into thick strips
50ml olive oil
2 fresh red chillies, seeded and chopped
1 tablespoon chopped garlic
2 onions, sliced
600g carrots, sliced
500g potatoes, cut into wedges
2 teaspoons paprika powder
salt and pepper
1.8lt beef stock
chopped parsley

Method
Fry the meat in very hot oil, add garlic, onions and chillies, stir and cook without adding colour. Cover with the stock, bring to the boil, skim, add remaining vegetables, seasoning and paprika powder, continue to simmer until the vegetables are cooked. Garnish with chopped parsley.

Dramatic clouds over Port Stephens palinkey, where newly slaughtered beef is hung. (Above)

Falkland's wooden gate, with the 'Indian Village' in the background. (Right)

FALKLAND
ISLANDS

Distinctive diddle-dee berries bring a bright splash of colour to the landscape, flowering in October with many berries to be found in late summer and autumn. (Top)

Stark cliffs on the south west coast from Port Stephens. (Above)

Rustic hues of lichen and moss scattered across the landscape. (Top right)

The vanilla daisy can be found around Christmas time, you might smell the scent before you see the flower; and Port Stephens shearing shed pens. (Right)

FALKLAND
ISLANDS

Two eggs are laid in a nest made by piling up stones, pebbles, grass, sticks or anything the gentoo penguins can find, often fighting over or taking stones from other birds' nests. If there is lots of food, both chicks will survive. (Above)

Horses sheltering from the breeze. (Below)

A rock reminiscent of an eagle looks out at the 'Indian village'. (Facing)

Steamed Kingclip Paupiettes

Ingredients

4 kingclip fillets
fresh spinach leaves
freshly grated ginger
cocktail sticks

MARINADE

¼ cup extra virgin olive oil
1 tablespoon chopped lemongrass
1 seeded and chopped red chilli
juice of 2 limes
dash of white wine vinegar
1 teaspoon sugar
sea salt and pepper

Method

For the marinade, mix all ingredients using a whisk and reserve. Place the fish over a clean surface and lay the spinach leaves over them, sprinkle a little of the grated ginger and roll over securing each roll with a cocktail stick. Place fish rolls onto a deep glass dish and pour over the marinade, leave in the fridge for 15 minutes.

Using a vegetable steam-pan with plenty of water, cook the fish rolls for 5 minutes and serve with green Thai curried vegetables.

FALKLAND ISLANDS

Gulls nesting amongst the sea cabbages on Carcass Island. (Below)

Cerritos from the air. (Right)

A young elephant seal prepares to go into the sea; Common limpet (Bottom)

Strong winds blowing into the bay at Pebble Island. (Facing)

FALKLAND
ISLANDS

View of Marble Mountain with the dramatic red of sheep sorrel, found widely throughout the islands. (Top)

An old peat cart still nearly intact; Pebble settlement with pigs in the foreground; At the western tip of Pebble Island is Pebble Cove, where the semiprecious stones that give the island its name can be found; A fine silver brooch with Falklands pebble, made by jewellery artist Anita Trestrail. Most of her pieces are created in glass and silver. (Above)

FALKLAND
ISLANDS

A rustic store shed – you can certainly tell which way the wind blows! (Above)

Pebble Island, one of the larger outlying islands, at sunset. (Below)

Rhubarb Crumble

Ingredients

FILLING
500g fresh rhubarb
70g Demerara sugar
30ml brandy
zest and juice of 1 orange

CRUMBLE
160g plain flour, sieved
50g ground almonds
100g butter
50g Demerara sugar
pinch of ground cinnamon

Method

Wipe clean the rhubarb with kitchen towel. Slice into an oven-proof dish and sprinkle sugar, and orange zest, pour brandy and orange juice over it. Rub the flour, almonds, butter, sugar and cinnamon to produce a fine crumble. Spoon onto the rhubarb and bake at 200°C for 25 minutes. Serve with fresh cream or vanilla ice cream.

Upland Goose Carpaccio

Ingredients

2 fresh goose breasts
2 tablespoons sun dried tomatoes
2 cupfuls of fresh basil
juice of three lemons
extra virgin olive oil
freshly ground sea salt and pepper
100g sheep's cheese
toasted baguette

Method

Wrap goose breasts with cling film and roll into a firm cylinder, place in the freezer until almost frozen. Take out and slice very thinly, place over service plate as you slice it. Put sun dried tomatoes, fresh basil and lemon juice into liquidizer. Pour some of the sauce on top of the sliced goose and finish off with the olive oil, salt and pepper. Grate the sheep's cheese and sprinkle over. Serve with the toasted baguette.

Looking towards the shearing shed and the settlement of West Point Island.

Owners of West Point Island, Roddy and Lilly Napier with Michael Clarke bringing in their sheep flock. (Left)

Proudly British! Often West Point Island is the first port of call for the many cruise ships that visit the Falklands. (below)

An easy walk to the dramatic cliffs on West Point Island attracts visitors from all over the world. (Below)

Black-browed albatross swooping, soaring and gliding on the winds above the sea and their nesting site above the Devil's Nose. (Bottom)

Diddle-dee Ravioli with Orange Sauce

Ingredients

RAVIOLI DOUGH
1 tablespoon unsalted butter at room temperature
75g flour, sifted
2 tablespoons water
30g sugar
1 egg yolk mixed with 1 tablespoon of milk

FILLING
200g diddle-dee jam
100g ground almonds
large pinch cornflour
1 whole egg
zest and juice of 1 lemon

ORANGE SAUCE
150ml fresh orange juice
zest of 1 orange
1 tablespoon sugar
25ml Cointreau

Feeding black-browed albatross. (Left)

A boat trip soon attracts a school of Commerson dolphins. (Below)

Method

For the filling, combine all ingredients in a saucepan and bring to the boil, as soon as it boils transfer into a bowl. When cold, cover with cling film and refrigerate.

For the dough, mix all ingredients in a bowl and work to smooth dough by hand. Wrap in cling film and refrigerate for 30 minutes.

To make orange sauce, put all ingredients in a saucepan, gently simmer and reduce by one third over low heat. Let cool and keep at room temperature.

RAVIOLI

Divide the dough into two pieces and roll out on a lightly floured surface to form 2 pastry sheets of 20 x 30cm. Using a teaspoon, place little mounds of the filling in rows of three, 18 in total. Brush the dough around the mounds with the egg wash. Lay second sheet of pastry dough on top and delicately press down around the edges of the filling. Using a fluted pastry cutter, cut out the ravioli and place over a sheet of parchment paper dusted with granulated sugar.

To cook the ravioli bring 1lt of water to the boil with the peel from one orange and one tablespoon of sugar, cook over low heat for 8 minutes. Remove ravioli from the water with slotted serving spoon and arrange on large gratin dish, pour orange sauce over, sprinkle 1 tablespoon of granulated sugar and place under the grill until golden brown, serve immediately with whipped cream and caramelised orange segments.

The upland goose lays low on her nest with the gander watching close by. (Left)

Often found around the farm settlements of the Falklands, the vivid yellow of the introduced species, gorse, where it has been planted to provide shelter for livestock. (Right)

Curious moulting Magellanic penguins. (Left)

Black-browed albatross chick. (Below)

Pannacotta with Teaberry Parfait

Ingredients

PANNACOTTA

1.2lt double cream
2 vanilla pods
rind of 2 lemons
3 gelatine leaves
150ml cold milk
150g icing sugar
small bunch basil leaves

Method

Heat 900ml of the cream, add the vanilla pods and lemon rind. Simmer gently. Remove the vanilla pods and scrape the softened insides into the cream.

Soak gelatine in the milk until soft, remove gelatine and boil the milk, add basil leaves and let infuse for 15 minutes, remove leaves and return the gelatine to the milk until dissolved. Pour into the hot cream through a sieve, leave to cool.

Whip remaining cream with the icing sugar, fold into the cooled cooked cream and pour into 200ml dariole moulds or ramekin dishes, refrigerate for two hours until set.

Ingredients

TEABERRY PARFAIT

240ml cream, whipped
120g granulated sugar
120g egg yolks
90ml water
150g teaberry purée
120g egg whites, whipped
25ml Cointreau

Method

Combine sugar and water in a saucepan, boil and reduce by half, put aside to cool slightly. Whisk egg yolks for a few minutes, gradually incorporate sugar syrup into the yolks until double in volume, fold through the whipped cream and gently incorporate teaberry purée, whipped egg whites and Cointreau. Place in the freezer to set and mould as required.

Looking over West Point pass to Deaths Head on the north west of the West Falklands

Thai Style Mussels

Ingredients

1kg mussels
2 stalks lemongrass
2 cloves garlic, crushed
2 red chillies, chopped
60ml lime juice
2 teaspoons fish sauce
60ml water
2 teaspoons sugar
coarsely chopped fresh coriander

Method

Scrub mussels under cold water; remove beards.

Cut lemongrass into thick strips, combine with garlic, chilli, juice, sauce, the water and sugar in large saucepan; stir over heat, bring to a boil and add the mussels, cook covered for about 5 minutes or until mussels open (discard unopened ones). Serve immediately sprinkled with coriander.

Looking from Ram Paddock Hill on Carcass Island to the West Falklands and Needles rocks.

Falkland Islands Government Air Service (FIGAS) flies daily around the many smaller Islands of the Falklands. (Below)

Lorraine McGill is making cream for the many cakes that need to be prepared for visiting tourists. (Below)

Kelp gulls and their new chicks keep an eye out for caracaras flying above ready to pick off a youngster for a snack. (Right)

Wandering along the track to the jetty. Cabbage trees along the track originally brought from New Zealand seem to particularly enjoy living on Carcass. (Bottom)

FALKLAND ISLANDS

Rob McGill has an early start – Carcass is one of a hand full of places that still milk their cows. (Bottom left)

An abundance of prickly burrs to stick to your socks and shoes. (Below)

Breeding around penguin and albatross colonies, the mischievous and fearless caracara, also known locally as Johnny Rook. Many pairs of Striated Caracara breed on Caracass Island; this adult protects his nest nearby. (Facing)

FALKLAND
ISLANDS

Smoked Trout Linguine

Ingredients

300g smoked trout
50g baby spinach
6 spring onions chopped
bunch chervil leaves
400g fresh linguine pasta
olive oil

DRESSING
¼ cup extra virgin olive oil
juice of 1 lemon
juice of 1 orange
1 teaspoon Dijon mustard
1 teaspoon sugar
salt and pepper

Method

To prepare the dressing, combine all ingredients in a small bowl and whisk well, then season to taste.

Flake flesh from trout into large pieces and combine with spinach, spring onions and chervil, add half the dressing and toss to combine.

Cook linguine in boiling, salted water with splash of olive oil until 'al dente', then drain and toss with remaining dressing. Return pasta to saucepan and add trout mixture, stir for a minute and then serve with grated Parmesan cheese.

FALKLAND
ISLANDS

Saunders Island, named after Admiral Sir Charles Saunders. A British International helicopter brings in servicemen for a tour. (Above)

Breeding on rocky slopes and often having to navigate steep cliffs and heavy surf to go to and from their nests, these rockhopper penguins brave the elements to bring home food for their young. (Below)

The beautifully dramatic shallow sandy bay of The Neck on Saunders Island. (Facing)

Mullet and Mussel Pie

Ingredients

500g mullet fillet
2kg fresh mussels, poached and shelled
2 spring onions, chopped
1lt milk
100g butter
100g flour
1kg garlic mashed potato
egg wash

Method

Place the mullet fillet into ovenproof dish with the mussels, spring onions and milk, poach for 5 minutes, drain and reserve the liquid.

Melt the butter and add the flour, form a roux and incorporate the milk, stirring thoroughly until sauce forms. Season with salt and white pepper, combine with the fish and mussels and pour into a deep oven proof dish, spread the mashed potato on top and brush with the egg wash, bake in a hot oven until golden brown for about 30 minutes.

A rusting old cast iron trypot used in the 19th Century for rendering of penguin into oil; mounds with gentoo penguins nesting in the background. (Top)

Louise Pole-Evans turning out the cows near the Saunders settlement. (Above)

Wild celery, flowering from November to January. (Right)

The smallest of the crested penguins the rockhopper penguin is feisty and noisy, playfully washing in a rock pool. (Far right)

Lambs feeding on an artificial mum. (Below)

Using the same nest year after year, albatross make their nests of earth and moss just beyond pecking distance. (Facing)

Sushi Rolls

Ingredients

500g short grain Japanese rice
cold water
2 tablespoons sake
5 tablespoons rice vinegar
2 tablespoons sugar
2 teaspoons salt

Method

Soak rice in cold water, drain in colander and rinse out several times, drain for 60 minutes. Place rice in heavy based saucepan and add sufficient water to cover the rice, add sake and

bring to the boil; cover with lid and simmer until all liquid is absorbed. Remove pan from heat and let stand covered for 15 minutes. Using wooden paddle, gently fluff the rice.

Mix vinegar, sugar and salt in a small bowl. Transfer rice to large shallow container, toss rice gently with vinegar mixture and cover with damp kitchen towel until ready to use.

6 x Nori sheets
2 tablespoons wasabi powder mixed with
 a little water to form paste
½ cup water mixed with 1 tablespoon
 of rice vinegar
225g very fresh trout fillet, skinned and
 cut into thin strips
225g cream cheese
1 small cucumber, pared and seeded, cut into strips
100g pickled ginger slices
black sesame seeds

Place bamboo mat on a flat surface, place nori sheet shiny side down, moisten hands lightly with water and vinegar mix, using hands spread one portion of the rice over nori sheet, spread a small amount of wasabi paste across centre of rice and lay strips of trout, cucumber, cream cheese and pickled ginger. Bring front edge of mat up and over to form a roll, shape into cylinder, pressing firmly. Unroll mat to release sushi roll, using a moistened and sharp knife cut crosswise into 4 or 6 thick slices. Repeat to make remaining sushi rolls. Serve with soy sauce.

The largest species of seal, the elephant seal feed mainly on fish, squid and crustaceans which they catch by diving to great depths. Flipper detail. (Facing)

A young wrinkly elephant seal pup. (Above) Sea Lion Island is a popular tourist destination and well known to ornithologists around the world. Looking back to Sea Lion Lodge from the Island's east end. (Below)

Seafood Spring Rolls

Ingredients

FILLING

200g crab meat
200g scallops, chopped
200g fresh trout, flaked
50g spring onions, chopped
200g bean sprouts
100g grated carrot
150g thinly sliced peppers, blanched
2 red chillies, chopped
2 cloves garlic, minced
5cm fresh ginger, grated
dash fish sauce
4 tablespoon oyster sauce
2 packs filo pastry
200g butter, melted
soy sauce and plum sauce

Method

Combine all ingredients for the filling into a large glass bowl, cover with cling film, refrigerate and leave to marinade for 30 minutes.

Use two sheets of filo pastry per roll, cut into rectangles of 20 x 10cm, brush with melted butter, place filling on top edge of the pastry and fold over the sides of the pastry, roll over. Brush the rolls with melted butter and bake in a hot oven for 20 minutes. Serve with the soy and plum sauce.

Rugged coast-line of Rockhopper Point. (Top)

Track heading to the North East Point. (Above)

A memorial dedicated to the crew of the British warship 'HMS Sheffield' is nearby. (Above middle)

From the Gulch tussac grass looking back to Sealion Lodge. (Above right)

FALKLAND ISLANDS

The brightly coloured orange feet of a gentoo penguin. (Right)

With a breeding colony of southern giant petrel on Sea Lion Island many of these fantastic birds can be seen swooping past. When threatened they can squirt regurgitated food at their attacker and so are also called "stinkers", a giant petrel takes off; Marching penguins. (Facing top)

Additional recipes

Polenta Cakes

Ingredients

125ml vegetable stock
500ml water
250ml milk
255g polenta
20g butter
60g grated Parmesan cheese
seasoning

Method

Heat stock, water and milk in large saucepan. Add polenta, cook stirring until liquid is absorbed and mixture thickens. Stir in butter, Parmesan cheese and seasoning. Spoon polenta into bread loaf tin, pressing firmly, cover with cling film and refrigerate until set. Turn loaf onto board, cut into thick slices and grill on heated oiled griddle until browned.

Madeira Sauce

Ingredients

1lt sauce Espagnole (readily available in supermarket in powder form or liquid)
50ml Madeira

Method

Reduce sauce in a saucepan by half to form a smooth glossy sauce of pouring consistency. Add Madeira to reduced sauce just prior to service. Season to taste.

Sauce Espagnole

A typical espagnole recipe takes many hours or even several days to make. The basic method is to prepare a very dark brown roux to which veal stock is added along with browned bones, vegetables and seasoning. This blend is then allowed to slowly reduce while being frequently skimmed. Tomato purée is added towards the end of the process.

Potato Dumplings (Gnocchi)

Ingredients

200g plain mashed potato
50g flour
1 whole egg, beaten
25g grated parmesan cheese

SEASONING:

pinch of nutmeg
hint of garlic
salt and white pepper

Method

Place potato mash into a mixing bowl. Add egg, Parmesan cheese and seasoning, combine with the flour to form a stable mixture. Allow to cool and shape into tiny dumplings. To cook, bring water to the boil, add salt and simmer the dumplings until they float, drain well and use as required.

To make tomato gnocchi add 50g of tomato purée to potato mixture.

To make spinach gnocchi add 100g blanched and well-drained spinach.

FALKLAND ISLANDS

Roux (thickening agent)

A mixture of melted butter and flour, which is cooked to achieve varying degrees of colour.

Béchamel Sauce

Ingredients
50g flour
50g butter
500ml milk, heated

Method
Melt the butter over gentle heat, add the flour and mix well. Cook gently for a few minutes without allowing the roux to take on any apparent change of colour. Gradually add the heated milk stirring thoroughly using a wire whisk, simmer gently for 30 minutes and cover to prevent skin formation, use as required.

Basic Risotto

Ingredients
50ml olive oil
1 small onion, chopped
1 clove garlic, chopped
300g Arborio rice
100ml dry white wine
1lt chicken stock
100g Parmesan cheese
20g butter

Method
Heat oil in a large saucepan and fry onion over low heat until soft, add garlic and rice, stirring for a few minutes. Add wine and simmer until absorbed, add stock in small quantities to rice mixture and stir over low-medium heat until all the stock is aborbed. Add Parmesan and butter last and season to taste. Turn off heat and cover, allow to stand before serving.

To make pumpkin risotto, roast 300g fresh pumpkin in a very hot oven with a little extra virgin olive oil until soft, remove from the oven and mash flesh with a fork, incorporate to the basic risotto mixture when adding the Parmesan and butter.

Basic Sponge

Ingredients
6 large eggs
240g caster sugar
240g soft white flour
60ml butter, melted

Method
Grease, flour cake tins or baking sheets, sift flour and put aside. Place eggs and caster sugar in mixing bowl and whisk on top speed for 10 minutes to thick ribbon stage and until mixture doubles in volume. Remove from the machine and gradually fold in the sifted flour with a spatula. Slowly pour in the melted butter. Pour mixture into prepared tins and bake at 200°C until baked and golden. Remove from oven and turn out onto cooling wires and allow to cool. Use as required.

FALKLAND
ISLANDS

Diddle-Dee Preserve

Ingredients

200g cranberry jelly
200g diddle-dee berries
100g granulated sugar
200ml port
1 cinnamon stick
6 cloves
juice of 1 orange

Method

Combine all ingredients into a thick-bottomed saucepan and bring to the boil, simmer gently and reduce by half. Remove cinnamon stick and cloves, allow to cool and store in a well cleaned and sealed jam jar until required.

Creamed Potatoes

Ingredients

1kg potatoes, cooked and diced large
200ml Béchamel sauce
300ml cream
2 tablespoon chopped herbs
salt and pepper
300g grated Cheddar cheese
6 large sheets tin foil

Method

Combine béchamel sauce and cream in a mixing bowl, add chopped herbs, salt and pepper and mix in the potatoes. Spoon a generous amount of the potato mix on top of the tin foil and press sides up to form a bag leaving an opening at the top, sprinkle with the grated Cheddar cheese and oven bake in a hot oven until golden brown.

Other suggestions

TO COOK IN A BAIN-MARIE

Always use an ovenproof dish. After you place the moulds/ramekin dishes into the pan, fill up two-thirds of the depth of the dish with water. This method works like an open bath where foods like crème caramels can be cooked; also a bain-marie can be used to keep sauces hot.

REPLACING INGREDIENTS

The main ingredients used in the recipes can be replaced by others found in your area. For example you can use sea bass instead of toothfish and ling or monk fish instead of kingclip. Berries nowadays are readily available in most fruit stores. We in the Falklands have learned to be very innovative and creative due to the lack of additional ingredients and have never been held back – just use what you have at hand and available and adjust accordingly.

You can buy food smokers for home use, they are very simple to use and you can experiment with different types of products such as mussels, oysters, fish, goose breasts, vegetables and terrines. Also experiment with the different types of sawdust you can use and mix in with other flavouring ingredients like cinnamon sticks, cloves, fruit peels, vanilla pods, certain tree and shrub barks.

Above all – enjoy the taste of the Falklands!